C000225828

WY PLAY HOUSE

And All the Children Cried

By **Judith Jones** and **Beatrix Campbell**
in collaboration with **Annie Castledine**

Director **Annie Castledine**
Designer **Liz Cooke**
Lighting Designer **Nick Beadle**
Sound Designer **Glen Massam**
Video Design **The Walnut Partnership**
Voice Coach **Charmian Hoare**
Deputy Stage Manager **Zoe Newsam**
PA to the Director **Geni Hall-Kenny**

First performance of this production:
Courtyard Theatre, West Yorkshire Playhouse,
Saturday 19 April 2002

West Yorkshire Playhouse,
Quarry Hill,
Leeds, LS2 7UP
www.wyp.org.uk

Tickets and information 0113 213 7700

Yorkshire Arts

The Company

Myra **Sharon Maughan**
Gail **Gill Wright**

Other members of the company (sound and video) are
**Susie Baxter, Alan Cowan, Sue McCormick,
Gail McIntyre, Robert Pickavance**

THERE WILL BE ONE INTERVAL OF TWENTY MINUTES,
FOLLOWED BY DISCUSSION

BSL Interpreted performance: Tuesday 7 May 7.45pm
BSL Interpreter: **John Parker**
Audio Described performances: Wednesday 8 May 7.45pm,
Thursday 9 May 2.30pm
Audio Describers: **Pam Wells** and **Keith Pamphilon**

Smoking in the auditorium is not permitted. Please ensure that mobile
phones, pagers and digital alarm watches are SWITCHED OFF before
you enter the auditorium.

Company

Sharon Maughan

Sharon trained at the Royal Academy of Dramatic Art.

Theatre credits include: **Things We Do For Love** (Stage West Theatre, Ontario); **Arcadia** (Royal National Theatre); **A Doll's House** and **Adam was a Gardener** (Chichester Festival Theatre); **Out of Our Father's House** (Fountainhead Theatre Co, Los Angeles); **Born Yesterday** (Sheffield Crucible); **Plenty** (Liverpool Playhouse); **Filumena** and **Habeus Corpus** (Lyric Theatre); **Hamlet** (Tour).

Television credits include: **Casualty, Dial M for Murder, Enigma Files, Dombey and Son** and **By The Sword Divided** (BBC); **Heartbeat, The Organisation, The Main Chance** and **Huggy Bear** (YTV); **The Bill, Hannay** and **The Flame Trees of Thika** (Thames/Carlton); **Shabby Tiger** (Granada); **Inspector Morse** (Zenith Films).

US Television credits include: **Ticket to Ride** (US TV); **Ruth Rendell – A New Lease of Death** (TVS); **Murder She Wrote** (CBS); **McGuyver** (ABC); **Felicity** (Warner Bros).

Sharon and her husband Trevor Eve have their own production company and have produced two ninety minute films with Channel 4: **Alice Through the Looking Glass** with Kate Beckinsale and **Cinderella** starring Kathleen Turner in which Sharon also co-starred.

Film credits include: **Another Stakeout**.

Directing credits include: **Windowers Houses** (Chelsea Centre Theatre).

Gill Wright

Gill gained a BA in Theatre Arts at Bretton Hall College then spent the next five years establishing Pilot Theatre Company and touring extensively in new work with Major Road Theatre.

Theatre credits include: **The Children's Hour, Gaslight, Tokens of Affection** and **Masterpieces** (Derby Playhouse); **My Mother Said...** (Chichester Festival Theatre); **Two** (Theatre-By-The-Lake); **The Gut Girls** and **Jack & The Beanstalk** (Albany Empire); **Romeo & Juliet** and **A Family Affair** (Contact Theatre, Manchester); **Tell Me** (Newcastle Playhouse & Donmar Warehouse); **Jumping The Waves** (Arc, Stockton); **Lady Audley's Secret** (Lyric, Hammersmith); **Blow Your House Down** (Live Theatre, Newcastle); **Sleeping Beauty** (Theatre Royal, Wakefield); **Top Girls** (Theatre Royal, Northants); **Bazaar & Rummage** (Chester Gateway); **Undeveloped Land** and **The Life & Death of Marilyn Monroe** (Royal National Theatre Studio); **The Mother** (National Tour) and most recently **Something Blue** (Stephen Joseph Theatre).

Television credits include: Nanny in ITV's recent comedy series **Sir Gadabout**.

As a theatre and movement director, recent credits include: David Wood's **Babe, The Sheep-Pig** (Birmingham Hippodrome & National Tour) and the premiere of Pilot Theatre's **Lord Of The Flies** (York Theatre Royal, Lyric Hammersmith). Gill has been a regular visiting director and lecturer at Bretton Hall College, Welsh College of Music and Drama, Mountview Conservatoire and Goldsmith's University.

Sue McCormick

Theatre credits include: **The Mother** (National Tour); **As You Like It, Bring Me Sunshine** and **Still Time** (Royal Exchange); **Richard II** (Demi-Paradise Productions, Lancaster Castle); **A Christmas Carol** (Library Theatre); **Cyrano de Bergerac** and **The Ugly Duckling** (Lancaster Dukes); **The Fosdyke Saga** (Plymouth Theatre Royal); **Lady Windermere's Fan** (Gawsworth Hall); **Something and Nothing** (Nuffield Lancaster).

Television credits include: **Casualty** (BBC); **Coronation Street, The Ward** and **Undercover Customs** (Granada); **Emmerdale** and **How We Used To Live** (YTV); **On The Boat** (Bremen TV).

Film credits include: **The Parole Officer**.

Radio credits include: **The Past is Another Country** (BBC).

Gail McIntyre

Gail is Director of the West Yorkshire Playhouse Schools Touring Company. She has worked at Nottingham Playhouse, the Dukes Theatre, Lancaster, Spring Street Theatre, Hull and directed for various companies around Britain, as well as in Canada, Portugal, China and Russia.

Recent projects include: **Visiting Grandad**, which in addition to its performances in Leeds' schools recently toured Japan, **Stepping on the Cracks** and **Whose Shoes?** performed in nursery and reception classes, all written by award-winning writer Mike Kenny; **Head On**, a peer education project dealing with issues around drug abuse, written by Mary Cooper and developed in partnership with local agency Base 10; **The Eye of The Storm**; **Temperance Street**, an artist led, arts based activity exploring alcohol use and abuse within communities; **Living Stories**, an ongoing project of performances and participation supporting the National Literacy Strategy.

Current work includes a new play in development with Sichuan People's Arts Theatre in China which will go into production in 2003.

Robert Pickavance

Co-founder and Associate Artist of Communicado Theatre Company, Edinburgh.

Theatre credits include: **Educating Rita** (York Theatre Royal); **Romeo & Juliet** (New Vic Theatre, Stoke); **The Taming of the Shrew** and **Mrs Warren's Profession** (Royal Exchange); **The Owl and the Pussycat, Anna Karenina, Neville's Island, Hansel and Gretel, Norman Conquests** and **Christmas Carol** (Bolton Octogon); **Augustine's Oak** and **The Comedy of Errors** (The Globe); **Who's Afraid of Virginia Woolf?, Around the World in Eighty Days, Cyrano de Bergerac, The Railway Children, Two Way Mirror** (Lancaster Dukes); **Foe** (Theatre de Complicité).

Radio credits include: **Bye Bye Miss America High, Where'r You Walk, Daughters of the Vicar, Well of Loneliness, Clean Break, Nietzsche's Horse** and **Henry IV Parts 1 & 2** (BBC).

Television credits include: **Foyles War** (Greenlit Productions); **Gas Attack** (Hart Ryan); **Kavanagh QC** (Carlton); **City Central** and **The House With Green Shutters** (BBC); **Midsommer Murders** (Bentley Productions/Chrysalis TV); **The Colour of Light** (HTV); **How We Used to Live, The Story of Frankenstein, Emmerdale** (YTV); **Jock Tamson's Bairns** (LWT).

Directing credits include: **Antigone** (Communicado); **Not About Heroes** and **Look Back in Anger** (Lancaster Dukes); **Woman in Mind** (Bolton Octagon).

Creatives

Annie Castledine Director

Annie is a freelance theatre director. From 1987 to 1990 she was Artistic Director of Derby Playhouse – an historic period in the development of regional theatre.

Theatre credits include: **Man for Hire** by Meredith Oakes (Stephen Joseph Theatre); **A Wedding Story** by Bryony Lavery (co-production Sphinx Theatre and Birmingham Rep, Soho Theatre); **The Mother** by Bertolt Brecht for Visiting Moon (National Tour), and **Spoonface Steinberg** by Lee Hall (Oxford Playhouse and Washington, USA).

Radio credits include: an adaptation by Mark Wheatley of Raymond Carver's short story **A Small Good Thing** (Radio 4, Catherine Bailey Limited Productions).

Beatrix Campbell Writer

Beatrix Campbell is a writer and broadcaster, a regular contributor to Any Questions and Question Time, whose work also appears in The Guardian, The Independent, The Scotsman and academic journals. She is Visiting Professor at Newcastle University, Fellow of the Academy of Learned Societies in the Social Sciences and three universities have awarded her honorary doctorates for her literary achievements.

Television documentaries include: **I Shot My Husband and No One Asked Me Why**, and an award-winning film made with Judith Jones, **Listen to the Children**.

Books include: **Wigan Pier Re-Visited**, winner of the prestigious Cheltenham Festival prize for literature; **The Iron Ladies**, a history of women and the Tories; **Unofficial Secrets**, an analysis of the Cleveland child abuse controversy; **Goliath – Britain's Dangerous Places**; and **Diana Princess of Wales – How Sexual Politics Shook the Monarchy**. **Goliath** was adapted by Bryony Laverey into a virtuoso one-woman play, performed by Nicola McAuliffe and directed by Annie Castledine. It was performed at West Yorkshire Playhouse during a national tour.

Judith Jones Writer

Judith Jones trained as a social worker in the Seventies, working mainly in mental health with adults. Her work in the Eighties and Nineties brought her in contact with women and children who had experienced various forms of violence. Her work as a therapist confronted her with the legacies of childhood trauma, both for victims and victimisers. In 1998 she was invited to become a Visiting Research Fellow at the Leeds Metropolitan University in recognition of her contribution to feminist practice, activism and academic thinking. She has recently been invited to be an Honorary Fellow at the Child and Woman Abuse Studies Unit of the University of North London. She lectures widely both in Britain and abroad.

And All The Children Cried is Judith Jones and Beatrix Campbell's first play. They are currently working together on their first novel, and are soon to begin a new play, supported by New Writing North.

Liz Cooke Designer

Recent design credits include: **The Magic Toyshop** (Shared Experience); **Destination** (Volcano Theatre); **Les Blancs** (Royal Exchange); **The Hackney Office** and **The Spirit of Annie Ross** (Druid Theatre Company); **The Glory of Living** and **Exposure** (Young Writers' Festival, Royal Court Upstairs); **Spoonface Steinberg** (New Ambassadors and Kennedy Centre Washington); **Behsharam** (Soho Theatre and Birmingham Rep); **The Comedy of Errors** (The Globe); **The Beauty Queen of Leenane** (Salisbury Playhouse); **The Daughter-in-Law** and **The Guests/Goodye Kiss** (Orange Tree Theatre); **Cooking With Elvis** (Live Theatre and Whitehall Theatre); **The Idiot** (West Yorkshire Playhouse); **Better, Arabian Nights, The Promise, BAC** and **Volunteers** (Gate Theatre).
Forthcoming work includes **The Birds** (Royal National Theatre).

Nick Beadle Lighting Designer

Recent designs include: **Private Lives** and **Closer** (Birmingham Rep); **Sweeney Todd, Perfect Days, Double Indemnity** and **Cinderella** (Ipswich); **Inner City Jam, Heaven Can Wait, The Mother, Killing Time** and **Shirley Valentine** (National Tours); **The Guardsman** (Bromley, Tour and The Albery); **Hosts of Rebecca, Happy End, Song of the Earth, Art, The Devils, The Rose Tattoo, The Rape of the Fair Country, Dick Whittington, Sweeney Todd , Threepenny Opera, Hard Times, Aladdin** and **Cinderella** (Clwyd Theatr Cymru); **The Gift** (Birmingham Rep and The Tricycle); **A Wedding Story** (Birmingham Rep, Tour and Soho Theatre); **Mrs Warren's Profession** (Royal Exchange); **Breaking The Code** Chester); **A Streetcar Named Desire** (Bristol Old Vic); **Portraits in Song, The Mother, Habeas Corpus, Mrs Warren's Profession, The Real Inspector Hound, The Snow Queen** and **The Wizard of Oz** (Keswick); **China Song**

(Clear Day Productions Tour & Plymouth Theatre Royal); **Vita & Virginia** (Sphinx); **Angels Rave On** and **Anatol** (Nottingham); **The Alchemical Wedding, The Merchant of Venice, Romeo and Juliet, The Cherry Orchard, Racing Demon, The Rehearsal, The Double Inconstancy** and **Noises Off** (Salisbury); **The Life of Galileo, The Resistible Rise of Arturo Ui, The Herbal Bed, Arcadia, Amy's View** and **Pygmalion** (Library Theatre); **Suzanna Andler** and **Hedda Gabler** (Chichester and Tour); **Vertigo** (Guildford); **Watching the Sand by the Sea** (Derby); **Tosca** (Opera Holland Park); **The Marriage of Figaro** (English Touring Opera); **Canterbury Tales** (Garrick); **Old Times** (Wyndham's); **From The Mississippi Delta** and **Full Moon** (Young Vic); **Jane Eyre** (Playhouse); **Lady Audley's Secret** and **The Broken Heart** (Lyric Hammersmith); **A Midsummer Night's Dream** and **The Tempest** (City of London Festival); **Gaslight, The Piggy Bank, A Country Girl, Marie Lloyd** and **Perfect Days** (Greenwich); **A Better Day** and **Waiting to Inhal**e (Theatre Royal Stratford East); **You Be Ted** and **I'll Be Sylvia** (Hampstead); **Hymn to Love – Homage to Piaf** (Drill Hall); **The Guardsman** (Albery); **A Busy Day** (Lyric); **Women of Troy** (Royal National Theatre).

Glen Massam Sound Designer

After completing the ABTT Theatre Electricians course Glen became Deputy Chief Electrician at the Fortune Theatre, London and then went on to become Technical Manager of the Theatre Royal, Wakefield where he stayed for ten years.

Since 1996 Glen worked as Project and Hire Manager for The Music Company, returning to the theatre last year as Chief Sound Technician for the West Yorkshire Playhouse.

In a seventeen year career Glen has undertaken many projects, operating sound and lighting for hundreds of shows, concerts and other events. Design credits include: **Stepping Out** (West Yorkshire Playhouse); **Salt of the Earth** (Hull Truck); **Soldier's Tale** and **Goblin Market** (Trestle Theatre Company); **Brideshead Revisited** (projection credit for Charles Vance); the annual pantomime at the Theatre Royal, Wakefield.

The Walnut Partnership Video Design

The Walnut Partnership specialises in the design and production of creative visual communications through a variety of media. Established in 1984 as a video production company the business has expanded to offer a full range of media services.

The Partnership adopts different delivery channels depending on the nature of the audience and messages to be conveyed. The resulting solution can take any form from an interactive CD-ROM to a video insert for use at a business event.

Recent work has produced a number of live events designed to integrate alternative staging concepts with advanced screen presentation technology. Current clients include National Australia Group, HM Treasury and the Leeds Initiative.

ARTS FOR ALL AT THE WEST YORKSHIRE PLAYHOUSE

Since opening in 1990, the West Yorkshire Playhouse has established a reputation both nationally and internationally as one of Britain's most exciting and active producing theatres – winning awards for everything from its productions to its customer service. The Playhouse provides both a thriving focal point for the communities of West Yorkshire and theatre of the highest standard for audiences throughout the region and beyond. It produces up to 16 of its own shows each year in its two auditoria and stages over 1000 performances, workshops, readings and community events, watched by over 250,000 people. The Playhouse regularly tours its productions around Britain and abroad.

Alongside its work on stage the Playhouse has an expansive and groundbreaking programme of education and community initiatives. As well as a busy foyer and restaurant which are home to a range of activities through the week, the Playhouse offers extensive and innovative education programmes for children and adults, a wide range of unique community projects and is engaged in the development of culturally diverse art and artists. It is this 'Arts for All' environment, as well as a high profile portfolio of international theatre, new writing for the stage and major productions with leading artists that has kept the Playhouse constantly in the headlines and at the forefront of the arts scene. Artistic Director Jude Kelly is a leading and visionary spokesperson for the arts, proving through the work of the Playhouse how theatre can play a critical role in society and the creative economy.

Charles Smith Head Chef
Louise Poulter Chef de Partie
Michael Montgomery Sous Chef
Simon Armitage and **Linda Monaghan** Commis Chefs
Lee Moran Kitchen Porter
Caron Hawley and **Esther Lewis** Kitchen Assistants
Gail Lambert, Gemma Voller, Emilio Eguren, Katarina Brown, Diana Kendall, Carrie Edwards and **Kath Langton** Restaurant Assistants
Tara Dean-Tipple, Sarah Cremin, Victoria Dobson and **Victoria Burt** Catering Assistants*
Jennifer Douglas and **Kim Jackson** Coffee Shop Supervisors *
Malcolm Salsbury Bar Manager
Sally Thomas and **Jennie Webster** Assistant Bar Managers
Rosalind Aynsley, Helen Cawley, Becky Harmon, Alexander Malyon, Patricia McMahon, Nicola Milton, Emma Paling, David Sinclair, Graeme Thompson, Andy Turner Bar Assistants*

Company and Stage Management

Diane Asken Company Manager
Paul Veysey and **Karen Whitting** Stage Managers
Porl Cooper and **Zoe Newsam** Deputy Stage Managers
Sarah Braybook,Christine Guthrie Assistant Stage Managers

Corporate Affairs

Daniel Bates Director of Corporate Affairs
Kate Jeeves Development Manager
Rachel Coles Head of Press
Sarah Jennings Corporate Affairs Assistant
Philip Strafford Press Assistant*

Finance

Caroline Harrison Finance Director
Teresa Garner Finance Manager
Coleen Anderson Finance Officer
Jenny Copley Cashier
Susan Werbinski Payroll Officer

Literature

Alex Chisholm Literary and Events Manager

Marketing and Sales

Kate Sanderson Marketing Director
Nick Boaden Marketing Manager

John Polley Graphic Design and New Media Manager
Shirley Harvey Graphic Design Intern**
Kevin Jamieson Marketing Officer – Networks
Kellie Whitehead Marketing Officer
Emma Lowery Marketing Assistant*
Angela Robertson Sales Manager
Caroline Gornall Deputy Sales Manager
Lynn Hudson, Emma Lowery and **Mel Worman** Duty Supervisors
Carol Kempster Senior Box Office Assistant
Bronia Daniels, Caroline Dennis, Sarah Jennings, Maureen Kirkby, Rachel Margrave, Libby Noble, Sally Thomas, Joy Johnson, Pene Hayward and **Ben Williams** Box Office Assistants

THEATRE MANAGEMENT

Helen Child Theatre Manager
Karen Johnson House Manager
Sheila Howarth Duty Manager
Joy Johnson Assistant Duty Manager
Asha France and **Bik Yuk Wan** Administrator Interns**

Housekeeping

Doreen Hartley Domestic Services Manager*
Mary Ambrose, Eddy Dube, Harold Hartley, Michaela Singleton, Paul Robinson, Teresa Singleton, Hong Yan Wang, Sarah Wonnacott and **Dabo Guan** Cleaners*

Security

Denis Bray and **Allan Mawson**

Customer Services

Kathy Dean, Jackie Gascoigne and **Leigh Exley**

Maintenance

Frank Monaghan Maintenance Manager
Jim Gaffigan and **Martin McHugh** Maintenance Assistants
Shane Montgomery General Services Assistant

Performance Staff

Andy Charlesworth and **Jon Murray** Firemen
Rebecca Ashdown, Ruth Carnagie, Maia Daguerre, Jon Dean, Jennifer Douglas, Shaun Exley, Simon Howarth, Sally McKay, Hayley Mort, Jo Murray, Soazig Nicholson, Caroline Quinn, Alex Ramseyer, Genevieve Say, Luke Sherman, Jamie Steer, Tom Stoker, Devi Thaker, Mala Thaker, Tal Varma, Daneill Whyles, Jemal Cohen, Deborah Barker, Rachel Blakeby, James Whelan, Fynnwin Prager, Sangeeta Chana, Vinod France, Clare Kerrigan, Indy Panesar, Gummas Phull, Ian Woods, Kirsty Latham and **Marcus Stewart** Attendants*
Beth Allan, Jackie Gascoigne, Clare Kerrigan and **Jessica Kingsley** Playhouse Hosts*

PRODUCTION

Production Management

Suzi Cubbage Production Manager
Eddie De Pledge Freelance Production Manager
Christine Alcock, Production Administrator

Carpenters' Shop

Dickon Harold Master Carpenter
Philip Watson Deputy Master Carpenter
Jimmy Ragg Carpenter
Julian Hibbert Carpenter and Metalworker
Andrew Dye Metal Shop Supervisor

Paint Shop

Virginia Whiteley Head Scenic Artist
Donna Maria Taylor Scenic Artist

Production Electricians

Stephen Sinclair Chief Electrician
Julie Rebbeck Deputy Chief Electrician
Christopher Sutherland, Drew Wallis and **Melani Nicola** Electricians
Graham Naiken LX/Video Intern**

Props Department

Chris Cully Head of Props
Scott Thompson, Susie Cockram and **Sarah Partridge** Prop Makers

Sound Department

Glen Massam Chief Sound Technician
Adrian Parker Deputy Sound Technician
Martin Pickersgill Sound Technician

Technical Stage Management

Martin Ross Technical Stage Manager
Michael Cassidy Senior Stage Technician
Julian Brown Stage Technician
Matt DePledge, Chris Harrison, Nigel Solly and **Jason Williams** Crew

Wardrobe Department

Stephen Snell Head of Wardrobe
Victoria Marzetti Deputy Head of Wardrobe
Julie Ashworth Head Cutter
Selina Nightingale Cutter
Alison Barrett Costume Prop Maker/ Dyer
Sarah Marsh and **Nicole Martin** Wardrobe Assistants
Anne-Marie Snowden Costume Hire Manager
Kim Freeland Wig Supervisor*
Vivian Brown Wardrobe Maintenance/ Head Dresser

* Denotes part-time
** Internship Programme in partnership with CIDA

West Yorkshire Playhouse
Corporate Supporters

Sponsors of the Arts Development Unit

DIRECTORS' CLUB

Executive Level Members

Associate Level Members

Hammond Suddards Edge   **YORKSHIRE POST**

Director Level Members

Bacon & Woodrow
Bank of Scotland
British Gas
BWD Rensburg
Crowne Plaza Leeds
GNER
Gordons Cranswick Solicitors
Grant Thornton
KPMG

Lloyds TSB
New Horizons
Pinsent Curtis & Biddle
Provident Financial
True Temper
Thompson Design
Yorkshire Bank
Yorkshire Dales Ice Cream
Yorkshire Television

One Performance Sponsors

Singin' in the Rain

BTcellnet

Inscape Investments
The Comedy of Errors

Horse & Carriage

Singin' in the Rain

If you would like to learn how your organisation can become involved with the success of the West Yorkshire Playhouse please contact the Corporate Affairs Department on 0113 213 7274/5 or email corporateaffairs@wyp.org.uk

First published in 2002 by Oberon Books Ltd.
(incorporating Absolute Classics)
521 Caledonian Road, London N7 9RH
Tel: 020 7607 3637 / Fax: 020 7607 3629
e-mail: oberon.books@btinternet.com

A catalogue record for this book is available from the British
Library.

ISBN: 1 84002 271 X

Printed in Great Britain by Antony Rowe Ltd, Chippenham.

Authors' Note

After the experience of working with Annie Castledine and Bryony Lavery on Beatrix Campbell's book, *Goliath*, Judith Jones and Beatrix Campbell decided to conduct an experiment in theatre which was: to discover whether themes which in their experience seemed to be untellable and unwatchable could be tolerated as theatre.

Jude Kelly, Artistic Director of West Yorkshire Playhouse, agreed to support and produce such an experiment. And in spring 1998 five performers, the two writers and Annie Castledine worked for three weeks at WYP devising, improvising, writing, and discussing. The five performers were: Gail McIntyre, Elizabeth Mansfield, Sharon Muircroft, Olwen May and Gillian Wright. A further workshop followed in 1999, when the first draft of the play was rehearsed. The performers were Barbara Martin, Olwen May, Gail McIntyre, Elizabeth Mansfield, Niarnh Daly. Police and social workers, as well as Gail, inhabited this script. But it was decided that the questions arising from Gail's narrative were the ones we really wanted to ask. To ask those questions boldly, it was felt that Myra was needed.

A rehearsed reading of the second draft, with the performers Gail McIntyre and Gill Wright, was staged at WYP in May 2001, and it was from this reading that Jude Kelly decided to schedule the play.

Our thanks to her, to all the performers who took part in the development of this piece, and to Diane Asken and Kay Magson, without whom the work would not have been made possible.

Judith Jones and Beatrix Campbell
Leeds, April 2002

Characters

On stage

MYRA

GAIL

On video screen

CLERK
of the court

BARRISTER
for the defence

GIRL
(young Gail)

FOREMAN OF THE JURY

DAWN

BARBARA

FATHER

MOTHER

The play takes place in a women's prison, occupied by lifers and long term prisoners, during the parole board sitting and the fortnight of its deliberations.

The stage contains a table for the parole board. Behind it, in the middle, is a large chair with arms. On either side are two smaller chairs. This is where the parole board will meet the next day.

Also on the stage are two cells open towards the audience. The two characters will move in and out of their cells throughout the play.

MYRA comes onto the stage and sits by the table. She is rehearsing what she will say when she appears before them.

MYRA: That is why –

> *Coughs and takes a pencil to change the words on the paper, then looks at the large chair.*

And so I resolved to assist the Greater Manchester Police who had reopened the case of the two missing children... and to those who believe I am seeking some narrow advantage I would stress that I am in my thirty-eighth year of imprisonment, having only chosen to seek parole since 1997.

Looks at the papers and then to the audience.

It's important I get this right. I've got a reputation to keep up. A reputation. My work is, as always, clear, well-documented and very well-presented. It's only fair. It makes their job a lot easier. I wouldn't envy anyone having to hear my case. Might as well make it straightforward if I can.

Now should I mention my health...? Try.

Looks at the chair.

You'll be aware that my health hasn't been good this year… I've done my best in the time since I've been out of hospital…

To the audience.

Sympathy…not a bad thing for them to feel that. Sympathy for an old codger like me. It's the truth after all.

Looks towards the large chair again.

The facts are similar, as you can see, to the last board. The only difference this time is that our argument, supported by current European rulings, is that the government's decision that I should spend the rest of my life in prison contravenes the Human Rights Act.

Looks towards the audience.

When we meet I try to talk to them as though we are at a dinner party. There's no point in not being polite, intelligent, cultured. They've got their job. I've got mine. No point in not being civilized. I'm more than a match for them.

Looks to the chair.

My team and I will all be interested in your deliberations in the light of that. We've done a lot of work. I know you'll try and do it credit when you make your decision.

To the audience.

Then I'll stand up, put out my hand. No, perhaps not. Presumptuous. I'll stand. Wait. Be deferential at this point. Then a prison officer will come and lead me to my cell.

She walks out of the scene.

GAIL walks into the scene. She is rather arrogant, disrespectful. Then she looks around and explores the space. Something about the large chair makes her uncomfortable. The room is not what it seems. She shudders. She feels small and intimidated. She sees shadows, dark and frightening. She knows she cannot look closely to make sense of the shadow. She looks to the other side. She hears a sound of a gavel banging on wood.

Then, voices.

Then on the video screen:

CLERK: Regina versus Robert James Blackburn. Day three of proceedings. Call Gail Blackburn.

BARRISTER: Under oath, you told this court that for as long as you can remember your father, seated over there, has interfered with you and had sexual relations with you right up until his arrest the day before your fourteenth birthday. Sexual intercourse, oral, anal sex, according to you, day in, day out. Is that correct?

GIRL: He did it. Yes.

BARRISTER: Speak up. So his lordship can hear.

GIRL: Yes. He did it.

BARRISTER: Day in, day out. Are you asking this court to believe that this went on all that time, in front of your mother, your sisters and younger brothers, none of whom are coming to this court to support your story? Day in, day out, in a council house, with paper thin walls. Day in, day out. And no one else saw?

GIRL: They did. They did.

BARRISTER: No-one else saw because it did not happen, did it? These are all malicious lies because your father is attempting to control your behaviour?

GIRL: I never. I'm not lying.

Cries.

BARRISTER: Easy to cry now, isn't it? Crying because you've been caught out telling lies?

GIRL: (*Whispers.*) No.

BARRISTER: So why didn't you tell anybody? When this was happening day in, day out.

GIRL: I did, I told my teacher. And she told the welfare, when I was ten.

BARRISTER: What happened then?

GIRL: They said I was lying.

BARRISTER: Lying… Yes. And they were right, weren't they? You were and are still lying.

GIRL: No. I never. I never. And they believed me this time.

She looks to the shadow then looks down.

He did it.

BARRISTER: Speak up.

GIRL: What?

BARRISTER: Speak up.

GIRL: (*Shouts.*) He did IT.

FOREMAN OF THE JURY: (*Echoing around the space.*) Not guilty. Not guilty. Not guilty.

GAIL/GIRL: (*Together, on stage and on screen.*) He did IT.

GAIL shudders. Body is feeling uncomfortable. Takes out her tobacco and papers, rolls a cigarette and tries to compose herself.

GAIL: Come on girl. Get a grip.

I was sentenced to eight years for the manslaughter of my daughter Kylie. At first they charged me with the murder of both my daughters, but the judge said there was only enough evidence for me to stand trial for Kylie. They had nothing on me for our Maxine. He saw that straight away, Mr Justice Harlow. He told them at me committal, 'You haven't got enough to proceed with the murder charge.' Clever. Him. He's tried all the top cases. They couldn't get one passed him. 'Drop it,' he said. No messing.

Anyway, I did get done for giving our Kylie an overdose of temazepan and then smothering her. Mind, he turned round and told them straight that I didn't mean to kill Kylie but that I was –

Looks at the papers and reads.

– 'an ignorant and unfortunate woman ill equipped for parenting a young child.'

Now I've done two years already and the reason I didn't try for parole before, was that I was set on proving I was wrongly convicted. I had all these people supporting me, campaign groups they said they were. They thought it was terrible. There I was, it was five years on after I'd lost the girls, the boys were growing up nicely. I was getting settled and then, bastard social workers started sniffing around, talking to the boys and got the police to dig up our Kylie.

Looks up and sees a shadow.

But I've changed my mind. I've written to them and told them to take me off their list. I might as well accept it, get my head down and do me time. My solicitors said, best thing is say I'm sorry, which I am. Point out to them that I've lost everything, my kids, my home and my freedom. I've been punished enough.

Looks directly at the chair.

When Kylie died I was still in a state about Maxine. Losing two little girls in three years. And that bastard… bruising me, just for looking at him. That's what a wife was for, bruising.

Touches her mouth.

Lost the front teeth on my wedding night. It's a wonder any of my babies came out alive. Bastard. And to think I got wed to him to get out from that.

Looks at the shadow.

By rights, you shouldn't call it a childhood. Anyway, I've done my best. I've said I'm sorry, I go to chapel on a Sunday, I go to anger management. The screws have given me good reports, my personal care.

Touches her hair.

My lessons, the sewing and stuff. I've really tried, me. I saw the trick cyclist. He said I wasn't mad, though I was bad with my nerves. He wrote – (*Reads.*) – 'no evidence of mental illness, nor of personality disorder, but an unfortunate woman, operating at a level of below average intelligence, whose natural wit has helped her survive without support and who nevertheless presents no danger to the public.' Mind, bastard social workers say they think I'm still dangerous. You'd think I was a serial killer the way they went on. Never been there for me. That lot. Always picking on me. Anyway, I was quite offended actually, the judge ended up being rather rude himself. Saying I'd neglected the boys as well and stood by whilst the fellas carried on with them. He said he couldn't understand that a mother could do this. He said it wasn't natural. Bastard. Natural! What's he know about what's natural. He'll be at it like the rest. Judges no different from the lot of them. I know that.

He went on to say I should have me tubes tied. I shouldn't have any more children. Fucking cheek! But my solicitor said though its none of the judge's business what happens to my tubes, that it's probably for the best. He said, 'Think about it, Gail, for the first time you'll only have yourself to worry about.' I'll have to go along with it I suppose. I said I'll do anything. I've got a lot to make up.

Don't take any notice of what my sisters wrote: 'We do not wish our sister harm but it is important to those of us who suffered just as much as her to stand up for others who were cruelly treated as children.'

Then on the video screen:

DAWN: You did it. When she needed someone to get us up. Who did it? You did it.

When he needed us strapped to the table. Who did it? You did it.

BARBARA: When those dirty gits from the club wanted what they'd paid for, you held me down. You did it.

DAWN: Killing Kylie. How could you? What did it do? Make you feel big like him? Seeing kids with tears, seeing the scared little faces.

Did that turn you on like it did him? Did it? Did it?

BARBARA: You, you never have anything to say! What do you think our lives are like? We know what it did to you. It did the same to us. Me, every morning I get up at six. I decide. I'm not going to kill myself today. I'm going to put on my mascara. Make myself a mask, and walk through the door into the day, doing my job, doing no more damage.

At night I think: I got through it, I didn't die and nobody else did either. D'you know, I'd have taken your kids. It wouldn't have been easy, seeing his face on your boys, your hands in Kylie's. But I'd have done it. I would have tried to love them. And I wouldn't have hurt them. Kylie would have been alive.

On the stage, GAIL turns to look at the papers which contain the victim submissions from her sisters.

GAIL: (*Reads.*) 'It is no excuse. It doesn't need to make you cruel. And she is capable of great cruelty. She isn't stupid. We would be concerned if she were to be released early.'

She looks at the chair.

Look, sir, everyone can see that we all had a shit childhood. He got at us all. I blame him that we can't get on together. You'll see, sir. Let me out. Give me a little flat and a clothing grant and they'll be all over me. Don't forget I was the one who ran off the first time and spoke out at my Dad's trial.

Wasn't my fault no one believed me. And those two knew, and they didn't back me up then.

Looks at the walls.

Where were you then, eh? Where were you? Nowhere. Nowhere, nothing.

Her body is exhausted and overwhelmed. She looks like she might faint. She holds on to the chair and makes her way slowly to her cell where she is alone with flashbacks and body memories.

MYRA comes into her cell and puts a video into her television. She watches the images of herself when she was twenty, her trial, the crowds. She hears someone reading her account of what it was like for her during the relationship with Brady and during the arrest and trial.

GAIL turns to look towards MYRA and moves to sit on a chair near where MYRA is already sitting, having paused the television on the image of her mug shot when she was arrested. She switches the television off.

I was at home watching Cell Block H with Mum. I would've been about fourteen.

She said, 'Get them up, they'll be in soon. I'll get your dad's cans.'

I went upstairs into the little'uns room. And poked our Barbara and Dawn, 'You two downstairs. Now!'

Then to the babies, the boys, 'You fucking stay here, bastards. You fucking don't move or make a noise and you won't get hurt.'

I pulled a chest of drawers to the door to block it. Mum said, 'Barbara, Dawn, sit here. Get them off. Now.'

'Now get ready… You.' – to me – 'Gail, where's the lads?'

I said, 'Stinking bastards, let them stay up there, Mum, they'll stink the room out with their piss…'

(*To MYRA.*) She couldn't stand that smell. Next thing men coming in, uncles, my dad, his friends from the club, taxis, laughing, burps, car doors.

Her voice as a young girl.

'I'm feeling sick. I'm going to faint. Mum.'

She starts to puke.

Then she said, 'If you're in the club…'

She winces and holds her face.

Our Barbara never got the clouts I did from our Mum, never…

'Shut up. Shut its mouth.' All I've ever got, me. My teachers…doctors. Her… Him… My mouth. Shut…my mouth.

She touches mouth.

They never meant shut it… They meant: Open it and shut up…

MYRA: Men…they shut us up all right!…scare us, hurt us… Keep us stupid, tell us who we can be, whether we are mad, who we can love…what we can wear, who we had to hurt…

Like a lot of women in here you've not had much luck with men. You've stolen, watched, carried, cooked…cleared up…and now that lot. (*Nodding as if to the parole board.*) Making us wait. The waiting's very hard when you're not used to it.

GAIL: The nights are bad for my nerves. Days are better. I just clean my cell or have a fag with the others, go to work in the mornings, have a good laugh, take my mind off things.

It's a lot better than at first… My hair's come on a treat since I came here. They're training it to fall down the other side, said it suits me better. Some of them. They don't try…

Ugh… (*Shudders. Sighs.*) At night, my nerves, they're terrible. Ugh. (*Shudders.*) I was telling Carol on the other wing… She worked on the streets in Nottingham, she said to me, 'Darkness is my friend.' I suppose it is in her line of work. We're all different, aren't we?

MYRA: And sleep?

GAIL: My body just can't settle – it's like everything that's ever gone in there, starts coming out, from everywhere. My back passage, it's on fire. I'm sweating. I can see him. Always him. Creatures coming into me.

She stands up, can't sit.

My heart. It beats so fast. Can't get my breath. I'm going to choke. The smells, lager, fags, sweat, his sweat, the visitors.

Then I think of the babies, the little ones. Oh, that's good, the little ones.

She looks at MYRA.

I'm telling you things I've never told myself…the babies, that's a good feeling, it's their faces, their fright I suppose. Makes me feel like I could do

29

anything, anyone. That eases it, the fear...turns me on. Then I'll come...and oh God...some sleep...

She turns and gets into bed, pulls up the covers.

MYRA: (*Shaking her head.*) Power, pleasure, from a kid's fear...what kind of woman feels that?

MYRA puts on her personal stereo, plays Callas singing Bellini's 'Casta Diva'.

Darkness.

I've missed a couple of days.

GAIL: Thought you'd deserted me, like my sisters... Just as we were getting friendly. Well, my personality and good looks must have brought you back.

MYRA: Well something did... It's finished then.

GAIL: Learning that...sewing, crocheting... I like that. Never could before, even at school... The sewing could have come in handy when we did the videoing. Some of the punters liked dressing up – so I had to get the costumes from the hire place – we put the charge on top, expenses... Up that bloody High Street carrying those bags. Some of them were heavy. If they were mock fur, or medieval... One punter liked the Lancelot suit... Awkward shape to carry...

Waiting at the taxi rank at the precinct... I'd see Linda sweeping the front of the chippy 'What are you loaded up with – are you doing sewing for the Paki factory?' she'd say. I'd say, 'No, I can't sew. It's for him.' She'd know not to ask any more. Bloody taxi queues. Kids screaming. Rain, hungry. Buggy broke, he wouldn't get me another. I said it's expenses – I wheel the heavy ones on that. That's why the frame broke – 'Expenses, you stupid cow,' he said. Like a horse I was. All he was bothered about was his cans and his fags… they don't care about us…

She remembers, sees shadows towards the back of the stage. She hears voices.

FATHER: Shut her mouth. I've told you as well. I want the girls sorted. You'll answer to me if she is in the club. I've told you get rid of it.

MOTHER: She didn't tell me until it was too late. (*Turns to GAIL.*) You shut up bastard.

GAIL: (*In a girl's voice.*) No Mum don't let him put me in the belts. Don't let him look up there. Mum… Mum… Ooww. (*Holds her face.*)

MOTHER: Let your father look, hurry up, get it over. Shut up.

GAIL: Mum, Dad. No. No. No.

MOTHER: Right, lady. You keep your mouth shut. You landed your father in it before. That happens again and he'll kill you.

GAIL: I don't care. Kill me. Kill me.

A crack sound.

No. No, I won't tell. I won't.

MOTHER: You'd better hope it's a juicy little girl. The only good thing out of this for all of us is another girl.

MYRA is remembering a voice she hasn't heard for a long time –

CHILD: (*Voice off.*) I want to see Mummy... I want to see Mummy... I have to go because I'm going out with my Mummy... I cannot breathe... Why... What are you going to do with me... What are you going to do with me... I want to see Mummy... I want to see Mummy...

GAIL: (*Screams, hyperventilates, has panic attack, then gets hold of herself. Looks back at MYRA who is looking very uncomfortable.*) Put that nice singing on. Calms me... takes my mind off things.

MYRA puts Callas on her tape machine.

MYRA: You're still upset by your sisters aren't you? They gave you a hard time.

GAIL: I'm upset by a lot of things. They don't know – it's like I'm a monster; they don't know what I lived through. It's like I was a prostitute and a pimp... But they did start me thinking. I couldn't go on saying I was innocent. They did make me think...

MYRA: Women are never 'innocent'. So what crimes are you guilty of? Manslaughter? Indecency? Transgressing women's natural role and instincts?

GAIL: I'm guilty because I feel guilty. When I think about it I've never ever felt anything else. Shouldn't have had kids me... Mind, I wasn't any worse than a lot of people. I just got caught. Unlucky, me. I never had a chance did I?

MYRA: I think I believe we all have a chance. I do not believe anybody is born bad. It is what we make of our circumstances. And for women of course our choices are more limited. But I think I disagree with your concept of 'never having a chance'.

You think your childhood meant that your journey to this place was somehow inevitable.

GAIL: Well there's got to be answers… We don't just end up here.

MYRA: I am not like you. I was not treated harshly as a child when you consider the time and the place. Neither was I without love.

My Gran, my Mother, though I know that they cared for me, were somehow unable to speak of it or even show it. We lived in a silent world of nods and sighs. They held themselves as if feeling and touching put them in danger. For in their eyes, everything hurt them: poverty, and men, each other.

To those who say that society is losing its way, casting aside respect, obedience, morality, I say look at my so-called respectable childhood. The fifties weren't all Jean Metcalfe and Uncle Mac.

My mother never had a new coat… She made do with a coat given to her by the doctor's wife whose cleaning she did and whose children she cared for. And such gratitude…humiliating… She once told me that she would receive a pair of stockings, Aristoc American Tan, as a reward for letting my father, whom I despised, have sex with her. When I returned home from my grandmother's at weekends I would hear banging from my parents' bedroom. 'No,' she'd say, 'Enough.' Then a slap, then silence. Next morning she would come down to the scullery, and hurry about her household tasks, hiding the bruise on her face and holding herself by her stomach as if nauseous. She would avoid my gaze as if my very presence made her feel ashamed. So it is easy to see why my generation grew up thinking that respectability was a sham, and refused to accept that sex was shameful. When I was old enough to have my own feelings and question this pessimistic view I vowed that I would never wear that look upon my face. So you see my 'excuses' derive from my sense of outrage at what lay before me…it doesn't give the answer.

She turns and puts her personal stereo on: 'Dos Gardenias' from Buena Vista Social Club.

GAIL: (*She shouts from her cell.*) The things you talk about, sex, desire…orgasms… You can get your mouth round anything you… You never get embarrassed?

I've never thought like you about sex… I can't remember when I had fully-sex, you know properly… You know, 'cos I wanted… Shameful? Who knows? It's just how it was, how it is. Something we had to do. Then marriage. I thought marriage was about hard work, broken jaws, babies and being got at all the time… Sex and family, sex and getting bashed, sex and marriage (*Sings.*) go together like a horse and carriage…

I thought when I came in here…that's the last pair of underpants I've got to wash in a while… That was a release for me… I know I'm not perfect, but I had no help.

VOICES: (*Other prisoners, off.*) Shut it Blackburn!
Give it a rest. Slag!
Didn't think they wore underpants in your gaff!
Miss. Tell her Miss!

GAIL: I'm not as bad as my Mum. I laughed when she died. Laughed. Had six cans of XXXX. Best day of my life. She hated me, she'd say, 'These are naice things, this is what girls do.' She'd hold me down and use her fingers before he put it in. And *He did it.*

The worst thing, when I was about seven. She said I had to *do it.* I didn't want to. He said, 'Sort its mouth.' So she slapped me across the face, caught my lip with her ring, and put my fingers in the door and closed it. It killed. Then *He did it.*

Then I was crying, they said better get to the hospital and get it fixed, could be broken.

Do you know what they did?

Called a taxi – it was Ray driving – and said, 'Get her to hospital and pick her up.' I don't think they paid him. He got something else did Ray.

They let me go on my own and come back on my own. I felt so stupid and that my Mum wasn't with me, told the nurses Ray was my uncle. I had to pay for that.

Touches her mouth.

CHILD: (*Voice off, which MYRA can hear.*) I want to see Mummy… I want to see Mummy… I have to go because I'm going out with my Mummy… I cannot breathe… Why… What are you going to do with me… What are you going to do with me… I want to see Mummy…
I want to see Mummy…

GAIL: Still he was better than they were.

Holds her mouth, retches as if being sick.

MYRA: Have a drink of water. Take some deep breaths…

GAIL: (*Drinks then breathes deeply.*) Never before. Never told anyone that before… Fancy that. These last few days all these things that keep coming into my head. It's like somebody's set something off that's never going to stop.

She holds head.

It's, like, frightening… But as well it's, like, exciting. D'you know what I mean? I don't think I want it to stop.

I'm not having you thinking I don't think. I do, I work things out. I'm not stupid. No good at school, but not stupid. It's taken me a long time but I'm working things out.

MYRA: Being in here you have time…away from it all. If you want to, you do work things out. Not that anyone here helps you. Keep your head down and say nothing. That's their motto. You come from nowhere to nothing. It's not taken you very long. I admire that, I really do. Some never do it. Some take half a lifetime.

But even so I don't like where your thinking takes us. You've had it hard, no-one can deny that. But your choices…that husband…neglecting your kids… There are women in here for protecting their kids. They've stood up to judges, who force them to take their kids to see their ex-husbands, even if they are rapists. There's others who steal, who go on the streets for their kids…choices…bad ones sometimes, but choices that hurt them not their kids.

GAIL: Don't you think badly of me. You sit there, listening, watching, pretending to like me but you don't know me. You don't know what it was like. I tried. I always tried. The girls they always got it. That's how it was, that's how it is. The girls. They can't be saved... Just did what I could for the boys. But the girls will get done anyway by their dads, their brothers, grandads...

Men. Think they own them. Right up to their insides. They'll always get us, right inside. (*Body creases up.*) Girls are different. My Mum used to say we're made for sex. She'd put on a posh voice when she was doing it. She used to say to us, 'These are naice things, naice things.'

She looks towards the shadows.

She used to tell us: 'Ay was born on the same day as Princess Margaret Rose. It's our birthday today. That's why my mother called me Rose.' When I was little I thought that made her important. Like as if she knew her. Not only when I was little. It was only when I was in here I began to think. You know Della, the one who's a laugh, organises bingo and quizzes for Saturday association? Well, this one... What it was... She put all these pictures of stars and royalty on a board... About fifty she had. The POs had brought her old *Hellos* and *OKs*. We all had to say who they were. I got loads of them. I've always been good at stars... When I used to go to the hire place and wait for the clothes, Janet the manager used to get *Hello*, she used to let me read it while she was getting things ready. I wasn't a bad reader, to say I was thick at school... Princess Elizabeth of Somewhere Foreign *invaites* you into her home. I got to know the lot of them. Anyway me, Carol and Shell all got thirty-two right. The others were far behind us. With eighteen and nine. So Della, who said she'd already thought something like that might happen, said, 'We'll solve it by seeing if any of the winners shares a birthday with a star. They'll be the winner.' Anyway, you'll never guess, I was the same as Wendy Richard – that's Pauline off *EastEnders* – and one of the late Princess Grace's daughters. That meant I won because I had two. Shell was the same as the Archbishop of Canterbury and Carol was the same as Celine Dion. So I won. I got a bottle of Nivea hand cream. That night, when the cell door closed, my mind was buzzing...all night I thought and thought... Just because my birthday is the same as Pauline off *EastEnders* and the late Princess Grace's daughters doesn't mean I'm anybody special. I'm still locked up in this fucking cell. For once I wished my mother wasn't dead so I could look her in the eye and say, 'So what if you were born the same day as Princess Margaret? So what that every time you had a birthday you'd say, "Oh, Ay expect she's out riding this morning before she goes for her presents. She'll have had naice things, a naice bunch of flowers from Roddy or perhaps a potted plant...".'

(*To MYRA.*) That was aimed at our Dad who didn't believe in birthdays except his. Then I thought. So fucking what, that you were born on the same day. Doesn't mean anything. Just another thing to scare us with. When I saw Princess fucking Margaret in the papers, up to when I came in here, it was just something else to make me feel cut off. Like she knew what was happening – another person who couldn't save us.

MYRA: It's her, isn't it, your mother, who gets to you? But when I hear you, all you had to put up with, it's him I think about. What about him?

GAIL: Yes well you, you always see them as worse, don't you...but she was worst in my eyes... Him, yes he was evil but I blame her, she was my mother...a woman, they are supposed to care for you...even after what I went through I knew that. I knew that as a sister before I was a mother...even I had feelings... Boys were brought up to be hard, cruel... I didn't want that for my baby brothers. I moved that cupboard in front of the door, to stop them. I got the strap across my face for that... Turns out it's a waste of time, he'd done them already. Nobody could save anybody... I knew that my kids were going to be fucked the moment they fell out of me. Not a thing I could do about it. They were going to be hit, burnt, strapped, got at...

CHILD: (*Voice off, which MYRA can hear.*) I want to see Mummy... I want to see Mummy... I have to go because I'm going out with my Mummy... I cannot breathe... Why... What are you going to do with me... What are you going to do with me... I want to see Mummy ...I want to see Mummy...

MYRA: Maybe that's what she felt? Powerless, frightened, men do these things...and there's nothing you can do...

GAIL: Felt! Her? She felt nothing, nothing. And with me she wasn't powerless. I thought she ruled the world... I've never thought of what she felt about him... I can't see her being frightened... I just can't see it... None of things the psychiatrists say fit her... She knew...she saw...she did it too... That makes her as bad in my eyes... But I've never thought about her being frightened of him... Anyway if that's your theory, come back here. Come on then, what about you? What made you frightened?

MYRA: (*Moving back to the chair.*) Me...well according to the psychiatrists, 'I have a remarkable capacity to tolerate violence and fear.' A highly qualified man, who had never interviewed me, but who saw my intermittent letters to the press, took me at face value and thought he could read my mind. Right little Cracker he was. But to be fair it is only in recent times that I have even begun to accept that I was ever fearful. The late fifties seemed to offer a girl like me, clever but unschooled, an escape. Office job...a decent wage...learning to drive a car... My mission was to escape and to be fearless. And so I formed an approach to men, which I believed would serve me well. I resolved that even if a man beat me, betrayed me – my experience told me that that was what men did to women – I would not be cowed. And furthermore I would have pleasure. The reading, which I had maintained through my schooldays, and during my first months of employment was chosen for its focus on passion. Not for me the ladies romances delivered to my mother by the *Boots* travelling library, stories of sexless, wimpish women. No, for me it was passion. Not servicing the lust of a man, but having my own passion, never wearing fear upon my face. This mission became my life. To be hard, fearless, was how I had to be. In fact it is only recently that this picture of myself has been challenged.

I remember when I was young, as soon as we heard the first raised voice and the inevitable sound of fighting, we used to rush in and my Gran would hit him with a rolled up newspaper and I'd cling on to his legs and try and get him off my mother. This always resulted in my being kicked out of the way or slapped or even punched. And this is what the top man cited as evidence of my 'capacity to tolerate violence'. That made me think. It is true that it is hard for me to remember being frightened. My concern at the time was for my mother and to hide my tears, which I saved for later. But recently I have remembered those tears, and the unbearable wrenching feeling of panic in my guts when I heard him shouting. So my strategies, I now see, were about self-preservation, from humiliation and from feelings. That is it. And the need to align myself with someone who could give me passion and most important of all, power.

GAIL: Listening to you – it's like listening to one of those documentaries on the BBC, as if you know the world is waiting to listen to you… So what went wrong with the mission?

MYRA: Wrong man and me… I went wrong

She looks uncomfortable. She puts her personal stereo on: Beethoven's Late Quartet (A Minor).

Darkness.

MYRA: You're looking preoccupied today, something on your mind?

GAIL: It never shuts down, my mind. They lock you up in here, shut everything down, then your mind keeps on. It's like I've said before, I want answers. When I first came, they told me to try religion. Try anything me. Some of them down at that Chapel

are like a bunch of Mother Teresas, up and down
like a bride's nightie… They'll do themselves
damage. Didn't help me. No, talking to
you…especially after our Barbara and Dawn set me
off…my mind's exploding, voices, screaming and
shouting, doors banging in my head. All the time,
something I see, something you say, I remember…
It sparks another thought. Last night I was thinking
of what you said about the way people take us at
face value. That began to get on my nerves.
Everyone has always thought of me as lowlife, as
thick, common, damaged goods. I'm not having it.
Because it's not how I can be inside. You know I like
that music you play. I like your words. And you're
right, I do make decisions, I'm not just hopeless.

*She struggles, trying to decide whether she's going to tell
the woman something. She rolls a cigarette.*

I want to tell you what it was really like… When I
had Kylie the first one who came to the hospital was
him.

MYRA: Stan?

GAIL: No. Him.

Looks up to the wall/screen.

I can't say the word… I saw his eyes. I saw his
fingers, as he trailed them up her thigh in the cot. I
saw him licking his lips. That's what's mad.
Everyone thinks I'm a hopeless mother but they
haven't a clue. I had to do what only a mother
would do. Even rabbits or dogs do it.
I had to save her from him… She was as pure on the
day she died as when I had her. He and I had never
touched her after that day at the hospital. Well I

always made sure I soaked my hands in bleach in case I did touch her. Nothing of me or him got to her... She was clean when she died. My beautiful clean baby. My angel...that was her, a sleeping angel... I thought, this won't be a case worth looking into... They don't bother about the likes of us, we're always raping, beating and dying... Every Sunday I'd go and see her in the cemetery, talk to her – the sweetest, angel that ever lived, out of me, a golden, good, sweet baby love, I breathed love for her, I made sure she was never touched...

MYRA: Christ. So you did kill her. Well I'll be dammed. So you killed her, fear made you kill her.

GAIL: I decided. To kill her.

That's got you thinking, hasn't it. I decided. You see, I wasn't hopeless. And I wasn't innocent either. That's why I decided to stop the campaigns, couldn't really let them make fools of theirselves. I decided to accept the conviction for manslaughter.

MYRA: (*Shocked.*) Not murder.

GAIL: Now I've told you before, darlin', I'm not stupid.
I may like you but I don't want to spend the rest of my life with you.

Let me put something lively on, it's like a tomb in here...

She puts on Gloria Gaynor singing 'I Will Survive'. Starts dancing.

Come on...get some exercise.

43

She dances around MYRA. GAIL's dancing becomes uninhibited, full of feeling and very beautiful. MYRA is uncomfortable. This is beyond her experience and her imagination.

Darkness.

MYRA: Not long now. You see it's straighforward with me. They know I'm not dangerous. I'm an old woman. It's whether they've got the guts to let me out. It's all politics in the end. With you, its not so clear. Anyway, you didn't get the publicity. Nobody has ever thought you were evil. They think you are thick.

GAIL: That's me! As they say as pigshit!

MYRA: You've got some people saying you'll do it again, some think you've been rescued and redeemed by prison. A bit of education and a smatter of anger management and you'll know how to steer clear of trouble. But I don't know. It's more risky than they think. Anyway, it'll not be long now.

Turns to her pile of press cuttings.

GAIL: No, and there's you with a mouth like a hen's arse. What's up with you?

MYRA: Nothing…just thinking. Confession may be good for your soul. I'm not sure about mine.

GAIL: Yes, I feel better. Talking, getting it off my chest. It does you good. I'll be alright, I feel I can face the future. I think they'll let me out. They can't fault me now. I was thinking the other night about when I get out. I'll get a little council flat. I'll get a grant from the social. I'm going to get me nets first if it's ground floor. A tele, a bed and I'll get some Dream Contrast for the wall. Now I haven't got the kids it's worth getting a colour I like. It's going to be mine. It's going to be clean. I'll have a coffee table with a glass top, with chineesy bits on it. I want my wall plates off his family, they emptied the house when we were arrested. And the kids' photos, specially Kylie. I can manage without a stove to start. I don't eat much. I can get something from the shop. A bit of ham or something to put inside a couple of slices of bread. I'll be all right. So what about you. If it doesn't go well for you, you'll just keep going, eh?

MYRA: This is just the beginning. We think the Board will find for me but the Home Secretary will block it again, on the grounds of the crime being so heinious that he can keep me in prison for the rest of my life. Then we'll go to Europe...

GAIL: (*Losing interest.*) Anyway I've been meaning to say, take my advice and lighten up – a bit of a sense of humour won't harm. People think you're stuck up, not like the rest of them, with your library jobs, your fancy visitors... You've got to think about how it looks...

MYRA: Thanks for the advice, I'll try and bear that in mind. (*Still looking through the cuttings.*) I hope it works for you. I really do. Living with all that inside you.

GAIL: Inside me...

Shudders.

My mother, she left me at the hospital on my own, just like before. Told them I was a little slut. She said the father could be one of six... Liar. She knew... fifteen years old... Like giving birth to myself... a monster... made by him and me.

I didn't want it. But the nurses said, 'A baby brings joy whatever the circumstances.' They said my Mum would come round. I didn't give it a name. It was *it*. The nurses said call her Maxine because the doctor that delivered her was called Max. So that's what they called it. When it came out of me I thought it would be like one of those aliens...off the tele. But no...it was just right. I couldn't believe it. I thought it was one of his tricks. 'You are mine right to your insides.' He was right. I was. He owned every bit of me. Every time he did it, he sprayed my insides. Then he'd say, 'Made my mark on you for today, my girl. Any other man goes in there, he'll know I've been there before.' So that's how I came to be so bad. So when that thing was born it had to be bad too.

So I thought, let's see, who's tricking who. I kept it beautiful, they were all surprised. Fifteen years old and a perfect mother. It was a good trick, because it did, it looked good...not smelly and ugly like me. He always said when he did it, 'You're heavin, you dirty little bitch...you make me want to puke all over your ugly face.' The other thing was I knew he'd want it. It was mine. So he had to have it. I thought, right, you have it, go on... I thought, he'll catch AIDS or something from it. I used to sit at night and hear him and just hope. But he didn't....he seemed pleased with himself. My mum said, 'That one's calmed his temper.' Every time he had it, I knew he was having me again. I tried not to touch it more than I had to… It made my nerves worse being around it. Then I thought I'll have to get rid of it…one last touch: I put the pillow on its head and held it down, put my knees on its legs, they were kicking, it put up a fight… I remembered that later when I did Kylie, and gave her some of my nerve tablets to settle her… That's how they got me for that one.

After, when the police came to see me about her, because of the bruises on the body, I said all our kids always had bruises. The police were nice, one of them said he knew some kids who could benefit from a few bruises. I got treated with kindness. Kindness! As if her death meant I had done something to be proud of.

MYRA: Why didn't you kill him?

GAIL: (*Shocked, as if she had never considered that.*) I wouldn't want any misunderstanding, I killed Kylie and I did it to save her… Maxine was to save me. Killing him, not possible. (*She shouts.*) He rules the world, don't you get it…? That's what makes me dangerous. I look at someone, hear a voice, a shadow and it's him, always him…

She looks to the back of the stage.

Always there. And because of what I've done it'll be locked inside me for ever. I need locking up me. We both know that.

A voice comes through the loudspeaker on the cell door.

TANNOY: (*Voice off.*) Gail, the Governor's got the letter from the board. You might as well bring your things. We reckon its good news.

GAIL gets up, picks up her possessions and goes out of the cell and walks into the audience.

Darkness.

MYRA walks into the cell and tidies it. Puts a tape on: 'Kyrie', Jose Carreras. Moves to the front of the stage, gets a chair, and faces the audience.

MYRA: 'Lighten up a bit,' she said.

Picks up an old newspaper.

So eighty-eight per cent of readers think that a 'Nazi Lover on a trail of death' should be hung... Six of you have offered to do it.

Looks at audience.

'Look at her,' you'll say, 'she's got a degree. That's more than her victims...'

Looks at another part of the audience.

Others will have theorized me, made a cultural study of me, I'm quite interesting actually. Some of you will need me to be released and rehabilitated because you are progressive and like me, believe in a society which allows redemption. You'll think, like me, even *she* is entitled to justice.

You might think that the Home Secretary should be interested in *me* and in whether I've changed and can contribute to society – I have and I can. I now know that for him, risk and redemption are irrelevant. No. Retribution. That's the core. Whether *your* need for retribution can ever be satisfied. Some of you might argue that we shouldn't even be in this conversation: that hanging would have been too good for me, too slow, perhaps too final.

Why him? A demented control freak. How could I have wanted him to be my lover? He was going places. Up, up and away. I had a lust for life…but I had no judgement. He *was* philosophy, music, wine. The burgundy sunsets on the moors, the first swifts taking my gaze right up, out, away from everything. All of it used to make me feel I could be and do anything. What a waste.

So, why? The education for a girl of my class must bear some responsibility. Our school trained clever girls like me to type, to make lamb stew and then cheese straws and sherry trifle in case you got engaged to a draughtsman. Judgement? No. So, when I discovered lust I went for it. I sought transcendence. What did I get? Lust, not for life as I later learned, but for death. Trying to escape the formica and potato pie which was my destiny and then this…formica everywhere…

I have known great love, a wonderful lover, devoted friends, even living in a place like this. My mother visited every month until the day she died. She always said, 'As far as I'm concerned, Myra, you're innocent'. Thank God she's dead now.

These are the facts. I didn't actually kill those children. But I taxied him, procured them and put them where he wanted, and then I watched. And like a good woman, cleared up afterwards, the premises, his clothes and shoes, the soil off the shovel…

Shudders.

I wasn't going to have grave dirt under my nails…
I gave myself to him and to his project, and to what

I thought was feeling. But it was his design. And I gave myself away, not to marriage, but to it, to him.

Those years of silence. What was there to say? If I confessed that I was his skivvy, merely an accomplice not his equal, his partner in crime, then everything I had believed in for me was nothing. *I* was nothing. So, nothing said. Hardfaced Myra, child killer, heartbreaker on D wing, saying nothing.

And I'm lying in my bed terrified when his letters arrived into my cell, bringing him: his tongue on the envelope, his fingers all over the paper and his hands, around my neck…grievous bodily harm, death threats, rape, sodomy. Seven years before I could stop those letters. Twenty-five years to start to speak.

So when Gail asked me what frightened me…

Shouts.

Him… He did it. Him!!

Body disturbed and uncomfortable. Puts on personal stereo.

I've been thinking about the names: *John, Pauline, Keith, Edward, Lesley Ann…*

It may sound strange, but there is an intimacy being with someone whilst they are losing their life. That Mother…understood that. She knew we shared something: her child and his death. 'Dear Myra,' she would write, 'did you kill my boy?' 'Dear Myra, please help them to find my son.' It was that Mother… 'Myra should stay in until she dies,' she would say on the documentaries. 'Dear Myra, yours sincerely…' She was just the kind of woman I didn't want to be, another sad broken mother. But after all those years she moved me. She had dignity… Like Gail, dignity.

What's to be done with us?

Looking towards where GAIL left the stage.

I've served my time, I've got friends and a home to go to, I've done a degree, I'm not dangerous, and I've shown remorse. That is the basis of my appeal to the people. But is any of this relevant?

To the audience.

You only know those childrens' names because of me. I could have run away, I could have refused to help him. I tried… No.

Yes, and he would have killed me for it, he would. I knew what he was capable of. I was his audience. Without me, he wouldn't have got the children, without him, we would all have had lives. Those mothers, they are common, tasteless, bitter. But they are entitled never to get over it, and neither should I. Forgiveness, redemption, and even retribution, they are all irrelevant. I escaped execution by weeks. We shouldn't be hanged. That demeans those who do it, and we shouldn't kill ourselves. We should try to live. We really should.

This must be my decision…

I shall stop appealing.

The music is Purcell's 'Dido and Aeneus'.

Darkness.

The End.